D1140948

Where do I start?

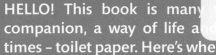

HELLO! This book is many things... companion, a way of life and in hard times – toilet paper. Here's where to find everything!

CONTENTS

WARNING:
PLEASE READ
BEFORE CONTINUING

YOGLABS

DON'T WORRY ABOUT IT

This book has ~~not~~ been approved by official YOGLABS technicians. Any injury or adverse effects arising from holding this book cannot be attributed to us. **PROBABLY.**

PFFFFFFT, DON'T WORRY ABOUT IT!

WELCOME TO THE DIGGY
DIGGY BOOK!

Find a chair, sit back, relax
and enter YOGTOWERS!

A MESSAGE FROM Yoglabs Officials

WHO ARE THE YOGSCAST?

... LOADING PLAYER PROFILES:

Little is known of the YOGSCAST from their early days. Check out the reports that we dug up from the ancient archive that was contained within a time capsule in Simon's garden (along with several crates of extremely stale jaffa cakes...).

LEWIS

Strategic prodigy Lewis has ████████. ████████████████. He likes long walks and ████████████ ████ with ████████████████

Text redacted by the CENTRAL DATLOF INTELLIGENCE AGENCY for your safety.

SIMON

Simon shows a natural aptitude around all physical tasks but struggles to follow simple, explicit instructions. He has however managed to successfully land all simulated missions – mission control have no concerns about him attempting a lunar landing.

Hannah has large forward-facing eyes and earholes, a hawk-like beak, a flat face and usually a conspicuous circle of feathers – a facial disc – around each eye. No. That's an owl. Our bad.

HANNAH

Duncan has a fascination and shows passion bordering on obsession around any form of volatile combustion. Please ensure he is not left unsupervized at any time: especially with Kim.

DUNCAN

Why is the sky blue? How many push-ups can a koala do? If you could choose a superpower what power would you choose? Which Star Trek captain are you? Is a biography made up of questions really a biography? YOU SHOULD ASK KIM!

KIM

Approach with extreme caution. Do not attempt to apprehend this man. Any information leading to the arrest of this man shall be duly rewarded. Notify YogLabs authorities immediately.

MARTYN

The domestic Nilesy (Felis nilesus) is a small, usually furry, domesticated and carnivorous mammal. Despite being solitary hunters, Nilesy are a social species and communicate using a variety of vocalizations including purring, hissing and growling. No. That's a cat. Our bad.

NILESY

ZOEY

Zoey Proasheck is the name, and videos are the game ... no wait, video games are the game. Videos about video games are the game. Hold on, what videos on what video games? I make videos about video games. Video-game videos.

SJIN

Kung-fu black belt and world-renowned prizefighter Sjin has never actually practised any martial art. No, his power comes from his moustache, now a symbol for happiness and prosperity across seventeen dimensions and three universes (not pictured).

Not much is known of the mysterious Rythian. It is said he was raised by jaguars, that he fought a troll horde and that his fingers have reached sentience, enabling him to play four games at once. None of this is true. It'd be cool if it was, right?

RYTHIAN

SIPS

Sips is a guy. A real guy, honest. When he was eight he ▇▇▇▇▇▇ ▇▇▇▇▇▇▇▇ and ▇▇▇▇▇▇. When he could walk again he ▇▇▇▇'d and then ▇▇▇▇▇▇. That's why he now lives in Jersey.
Redacted for decency's sake. Trust us.

When faced with a crisis do you:

a) Ignore it and hope it will go away?
b) Pounce on the challenge and beat it into submission?
c) Wait for a certain other Hat Films teammate to handle it?

You're the last one leaving Yogstowers. Do you:

a) Walk out and hope no one notices the door is open?
b) Pounce on the challenge and lock every door and window?
c) Wait for a certain other Hat Films teammate to handle it?

You're in an enemy respawn zone. Do you:

a) Set a trap and walk away from the party?
b) Pounce on the challenge and shoot them into submission?
c) Wait for a certain other Hat Films teammate to handle it?

Did you answer mostly A? I'm sorry. You're most like:

Did you answer mostly B? Congratulations! You pounced on this challenge.

Mostly C? There's no hope for you. You're definitely:

ROSS

SMITHY

TROTT

This is a story all about how my life got flipped, turned upside down. And I'd like to take a minute - I'll try to be fast. I'll tell you how I became CEO of Yogscast. In Bristol, England born and raised, World of Warcraft where I spent most of my days. Chilling out, grinding, levelling toons, all unbeknownst to Ye Olde Goons. When a couple of guys, after I harassed, agreed to come on The Incredible Podcast. We started hanging out and, at long last, I started living the dream with The Yogscast.

PYRION

TURPS

WELCOME, PLAYER! Now you've caught up on who the Yogscast are, it's time to visit YogLabs - TURN PAGE TO START GAME:

LIVE CAM LOADING...

Everyone loves a montage, right??

WHO BURPED INTO THE MIC?

Full of classy, tasteful artwork.

You'll often find Sips banished out here.

HE HALL OF SHAME

Simon needs SOMEWHERE to do his laundry.

CLEAN UP ON AISLE 3!

GREEN SCREEN of DOOM!

Which one do I look at first?

WHERE FOOD MAGIC HAPPENS :)

One of our personal dogsbodies, Lewis.

HE EDITING FEZ IS WATCHIN

20% YOU MONSTER FRIED CHICKEN

FREE DRUMSTICK!

WHAT DOES THIS BUTTON DO?

1 - Cleaning Supplies
2 - Annular Confinement Beam Control
3 - Pattern Buffers
4 - Canadian Organ Donors
5 - Electro-Shock Therapy Department
6 - Crematorium
7 - Complaints Department
8 - Sewer Maintenance
9 - Management Lounge
10 - Staff Offices
11 - Staff Break Room
12 - Medical Wing Reception

13 - Armoury
14 - Honeydew's Office
15 - Metallurgic Combobulati
16 - Atmospheric Reaction Ch
17 - Matter Transfer Hub
18 - Dark Room Storage
19 - Coffee Machine
20 - Break Room
21 - Coffee Machine Maintena
22 - Launch Pad
23 - Airship Construction Ha
24 - Holo Bays

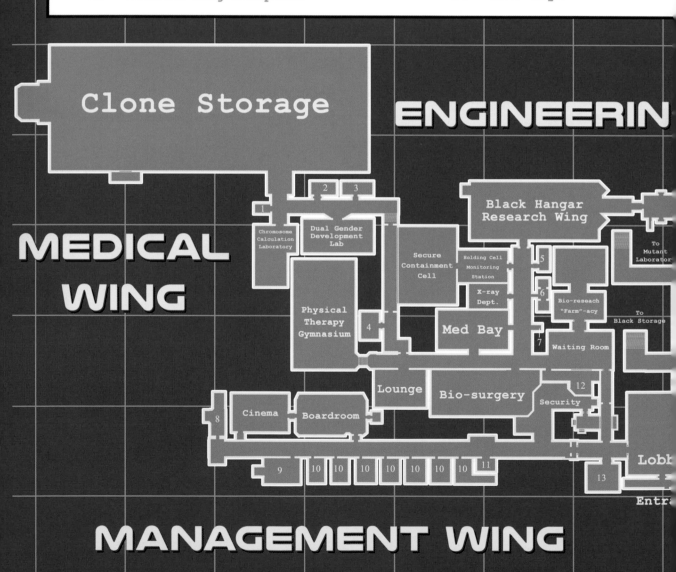

Clone Storage

ENGINEERIN

MEDICAL

WING

Chromosome Calculation Laboratory

Dual Gender Development Lab

Black Hangar Research Wing

To Mutant Laborator

Secure Containment Cell

Holding Cell Monitoring Station

X-ray Dept.

Bio-reseach "Farm"-acy

To Black Storage

Physical Therapy Gymnasium

Med Bay

Waiting Room

Lounge

Bio-surgery

Security

Lobb

Cinema

Boardroom

Entra

MANAGEMENT WING

Confidential Information
YogLabs Stargate mission log.

01/10/13 - Stargate uncovered in Deep Search III.

06/10/13 - Final chevron installed and SG teams formed.

08/10/13 - SG-1 sent to explore planet Rssumba.

11/10/13 - Firebase Alpha established.

18/10/13 - A final garbled message received from Firebase Alpha. After this, all contact was lost.

20/10/13 - Xephos and Honeydew travel through the gate to investigate and re-establish contact with the base. Sergeant Herp is the only survivor and the base is overrun by vicious alien bugs. The team barely manage to escape alive. Thirty-six researchers and nineteen soldiers KIA. Firebase Alpha considered a total loss.

21/10/13 - Rssumba is quarantined and the address is removed from the Stargate database. Sergeant Herp continues to receive counselling but his recovery seems unlikely. Bug specimens sent for further research and the mission is considered a success.

PRIMARY OBJECTIVE ACHIEVED

23/10/13 - Professor Bixby begins conducting his own private research on planet Aiesmba and labels it off-limits due to dangerous life forms.

26/10/13 - Xephos and Honeydew travel to Aiesmba to capture more specimens but discover that Bixby has found an all-women island paradise and labelled it as dangerous in an effort to keep it for himself. Honeydew befriends one of the indigenous women, which starts a conflict, disrupting the island's harmony. The ensuing chaos attracts the island's dangerous predators which devour the inhabitants. The team manage to escape and Bixby offers the surviving islanders his "personal protection".

27/10/13 - Aiesmba is quarantined and the address is removed from the Stargate database. Basilisk and attack-squid specimens sent for further research. **PRIMARY OBJECTIVE ACHIEVED**

28/10/13 - Bixby resigns from the Stargate project claiming he "has his hands full at home and can't spare the time".

30/10/13 - SG-2 sent to investigate planet Cuthula and initial reports are very promising.

31/10/13 - Contact lost with SG-2, Honeydew leads SG-1 sent to investigate.

01/11/13 - Contact lost with SG-1. Honeydew clone 42a created and sent to lead SG-3.

02/11/13 - All SG teams and 64 Honeydew clones are lost investigating planet Cuthula and Deep Search III is no longer responding.

03/11/13 - Honeydew clone 107 returns from Deep Search III rambling about unspeakable horrors. Clone considered unrecoverable and is recycled.

04/11/13 - Deep Search III and sub levels 42-65 sealed with ferrocrete.

STARGATE PROJECT ABANDONED

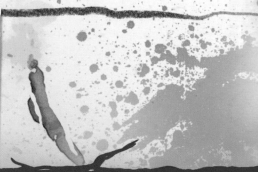

YOGLABS EVIDENCE 147

YOGLABS EVIDENCE 031

HERE'S WHAT'S COMING

predicted full
flux transformation

Will the correla...
match to that of ...

...icted complete
...rmation?
...ection continue, I have predicted
...s final Flux form. It is frightening.
...emember me?

DRAW IN
PUDGE'S
HOOK

? ?

ENTRAL
COMPOUND

VISIT DAILOF!!

NEW TO NOODLES?

HO
H

TRY SOME CHILI

DIG A HOLE!

FLY THE JAFFA CRUISER

-THE-
HAND

IT'S
A C
IT'S A WA

FOLLOW THE HAND!

WARNING!
WARNING!
WARNING!

YOU ARE NOW LEAVING YOGLABS. WE CANNOT GUARANTEE YOUR SAFETY BEYOND THIS POINT. KEEP YOUR ARMS INSIDE THE VEHICLE AT ALL TIMES. DO NOT LOOK DOWN. DO NOT PASS GO. DO KEEP READING.

PLEASE READ THE HEALTH & SAFETY INFORMATION BEFORE LEAVING THE COMFORT OF THIS PAGE.

BY NOW YOU MUST BE WONDERING –
HOW BIG IS THE YOGSVERSE? WHAT IS IT?
AND WHERE DID IT COME FROM?

WE DON'T HAVE THE ANSWERS YOU SEEK.

STEP INSIDE OWL ISLAND, YOGSEY
PENITENTIARY, SJIN'S FARM, SIPS' ROOM,
THE HAND OF TRUTH AND THE POINTLESS
MIND OF PYRION.

FRIGHT NIGHT FACT FILES

Name: Hannah	DOB: 6/6/1666	Height: 5ft 4"	Motive: Kicking monster butts
Name: Kim	DOB: 17/6/1887	Height: 5ft	Motive: Discovering new creeps

It's a dark and deadly world that you find yourself in – beware of the creatures that go bump in the night! There be monsters and there be ghosts everywhere … but do not despair! You are not entirely* alone, for Kim and Hannah's Fright Night Fact Files will prepare you to wage war against the fiends in the darkness.

THE FRIGHT NIGHT SURVIVOR'S EQUIPMENT LIST:

☒ CLIPBOARD
Use your clipboard for writing down each monster's backstory. In blood. Worst comes to worst, it makes a great blunt object for bludgeoning.

☒ CAMERA
Get those ghosties in frame and press "click"! Don't forget the selfie stick.

☒ FLAMETHROWER
The Fright Night survivor's weapon of choice.

☒ TORCH
To stop you bumping into stuff. Especially handy when wading through sewers, creeping into basements and exploring disused warehouses.

☒ SPARE BATTERIES
Essential to power that torch and camera. After all, you don't want to be there when the lights go out, do you?

* Except you are…

F.N. INC.

Name: Mr SOGGY THUMB

I.D NO: 666-579-391

Height: Unknown

Weight: Unknown

Origin: Military

Location: The deepest, darkest corners of your high school changing room

HISTORY:

Originating from a military background, Mr Soggy Thumb has undergone genetic experimentation to make him even faster, stronger and harder to defeat. This monster takes no prisoners and feels no remorse. He also stinks. Avoid encounters without putting a face mask on first.

APPEARANCE:

A giant, looming man, with bad personal hygiene.

WEAKNESSES:

Tiny spaces and/or lockers.

ATTACK TIP:

Lure him towards other military experiments, especially psychic ones loitering near air vents.

EQUIPMENT NEEDED:
☒ CLIPBOARD ☐ CAMERA ☐ TORCH ☒ FLAMETHROWER

F.N. INC.

HISTORY:

Born from the depths of the internet, Slender Man is the stuff nightmares are born from. He floats closer when you're not looking and ruins all your camera footage. If that wasn't bad enough, he's recently amassed an army of terrifying, blank-faced mannequins. URGH.

APPEARANCE:

Tall, thin, pale face. Wears a suit that's sharper than a London bank manager.

WEAKNESSES:

Lack of direct eye contact.

ATTACK TIP:

Hide behind a mirror and burn his precious notes. That'll really upset him.

Name: SLENDER MAN

I.D NO: 666-118-118

Height: 6ft 1"

Weight: Unknown

Origin: Message board

Location: Behind you

EQUIPMENT NEEDED:
☐ CLIPBOARD   ☒ CAMERA   ☒ TORCH   ☐ FLAMETHROWER

F.N. INC.

Name: JOHN DOE

I.D NO: 666-101-008

Height: Unknown

Weight: Unknown

Origin: Somewhere

Location: Everywhere and nowhere at the same time

HISTORY:

A difficult monster to spot, John Doe looks uncannily like a Fright Night survivor … apart from a limping gait, blank face and relentless groaning. This species of zombie tends to gather in large groups, usually intent on bringing about an apocalypse.

APPEARANCE:

An unassuming everyman. Who happens to be dead.

WEAKNESSES:

Incredibly slow moving.

ATTACK TIP:

Walk slightly faster than John Doe, and you'll be fine. Failing that, BURN IT WITH FIRE.

EQUIPMENT NEEDED:

☐ BOARD ☐ CAMERA ☐ TORCH ☒ FLAMETHROWER

F.N. INC.

HISTORY:

This monster may seem a bit peaky, but looks can be deceptive. When sighted in the wild, Madame Pale is a harbinger of doom ... yours, usually. Part ghost, part siren, she is almost impossible to kill.

APPEARANCE:

A floaty lady in a white dress with long black hair.

WEAKNESSES:

Cannot take criticism.

ATTACK TIP:

Throw mud at Madame Pale's lovely white dress to really mess her up.

Name: MADAME PALE

I.D NO: 666-800-813

Height: Unknown

Weight: Weightless

Origin: Onsen bath

Location: Down the end of your hallway

EQUIPMENT NEEDED:
☐ CLIPBOARD   ☐ CAMERA   ☒ TORCH   ☐ FLAMETHROWER

Name: **BILLY-LONG-LEGS**

I.D NO: 666-LV-426

Height: 8ft ???

Weight: Unknown

Origin: Desolate planet

Location: In the ducts
of your spaceship
somewhere

HISTORY:

It comes from outer space and is usually (if not always) bent on the destruction of you, your friends, your family and – indeed – all mankind. It may have acquired simple phrases or song lyrics from satellites sent out into space over the years – but don't be fooled! What it really wants to say is … "DIE, EARTHLING!"

APPEARANCE:

Leathery, dark skin, more teeth than a frenzy of sharks, apex predator smile. Slimy. Very slimy.

WEAKNESSES:

NO KNOWN WEAKNESS. Approach with caution or not at all

ATTACK TIP:

Nuke it from orbit. If nukes are hard to come by, attack it with a flamethrower, trap it in an airlock and hit EJECT.

EQUIPMENT NEEDED:
☐ CLIPBOARD ☒ CAMERA ☐ TORCH ☒ FLAMETHROWER

Owl Island

Deep in the Minecraft mods you'll find the secrets of Owl Island – a map is always handy!

Clearing out the bay

Nilesy's first Pool Shack

OWL ISLAND

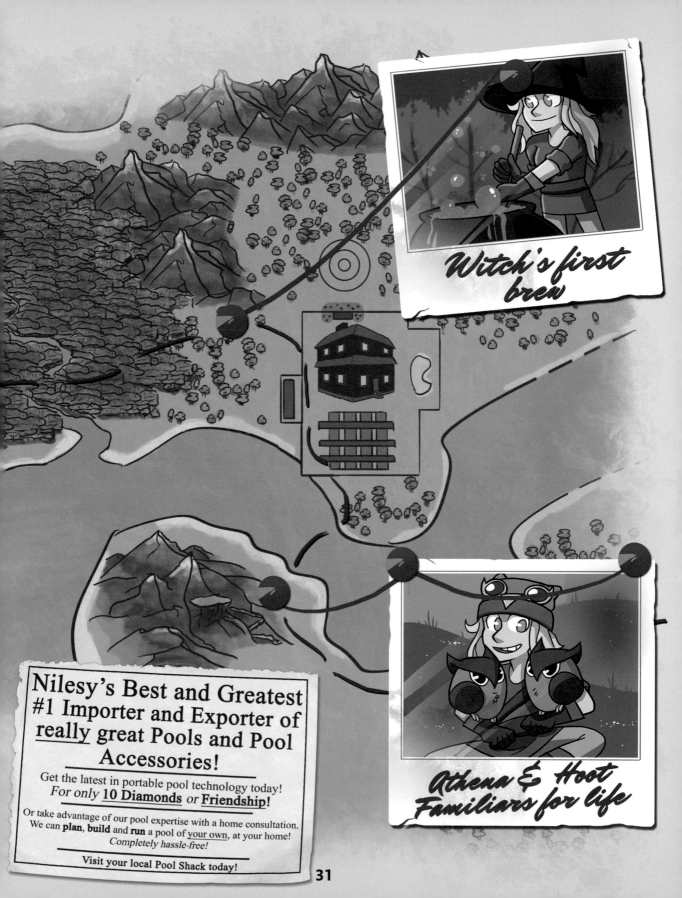

Witch's first brew

Athena & Hoot Familiars for life

31

DD

DUNCAN'S DRIVING SCHOOL

ESSENTIAL FOR ALL DRIVERS

FULLY LICENSED INSTRUCTOR*

1

2

3

4

5

6

The streets of GTA are tough, so you have to get tougher. Some important tips from Duncan's Driving School of staying safe and streetwise!

1. Pedestrians Crossing
Pedestrians are safe, so long as they don't cross you.

2. Law Enforcement
A life of crime would be perfect if it wasn't for all the cops.

3. Murder In Progress
Back-seat drivers have to go somewhere other than the trunk.

4. High Chance of Muggings
Money can't buy you happiness, but it will most likely get you robbed.

5. Road Rage
Rush hour is not a problem ... when you're ready with your mouth!

6. Road Justice
Dangerous drivers are no worry when you have your trusty bat by your side.

*No one at YogLabs endorses Duncan's Driving School, what he may teach you, or what he will say to you.

BREAKOUT!

Do you have enough strength to break out of Yogsey Penitentiary? Grab your duct tape, stick a file in your sock and get ready to rattle your cage! Convict Littlewood is using all of his wiles and resources to pull off the greatest escape.

No silly mistakes, no missing roll call and no soap jokes.

BUNK UP – Make a dummy and tuck it into your bed. Random cell checks can take place at any time.

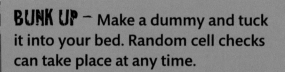

ALWAYS WATCHING – Study the staff rotation patterns before making a move. Remember, guards are **corrupt**.

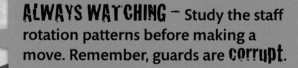

PRISON BREAK – If you do finally make it out, all you've got to do is fight off the dogs, pick the barbed wire out of your trousers and repel the electric fence. Easy-peasy. Right?

IT'S NOT A CULT

IT'S A WAY OF LIFE

1. CLEANSE YOUR EARTHLY VESSEL IN GOLD

AT OUR CHURCH WE WANT EVERYONE IN THE UNIVERSE TO EXPERIENCE THE GLORY AND MAGNIFICENCE OF THE HAND. THROUGH OUR GOLD CLEANSINGS, WE BELIEVE PEOPLE ARE BROUGHT CLOSER TO THE TRUTHS THE HAND OFFERS. (AVAILABLE AT SELECTED CHURCHES FROM 8 A.M. TO 12 P.M. ON TUESDAYS.)

2. CLEAR YOUR MIND AND SOUL

EVER FEEL LIGHT-HEADED AND TIRED FOR NO REASON? DO YOU FIND IT DIFFICULT TO GET EXCITED ABOUT WHAT THE HAND OF TRUTH OFFERS YOU? AN IMPORTANT STEP TOWARDS ENLIGHTENMENT IS CLEARING YOUR MIND OF DISTRACTING THOUGHTS, AND FOCUSING YOUR ENERGY ON SOMETHING POSITIVE, LIKE FOLLOWING THE HAND'S INSTRUCTIONS UNWAVERINGLY AND WITHOUT HESITATION.

3. SHOW YOUR DEVOTION

THE HAND'S LOVE IS ETERNAL, BUT IS NOT GIVEN EASILY. TO SHOW YOUR DEVOTION, WE ASK THAT YOU CREATE YOUR OWN GOLDEN HAND AND DISPLAY IT OUTSIDE YOUR HOME. IF ANY NEIGHBOURS QUESTION YOUR CHOICE OF GARDEN ORNAMENTS, THIS IS A GREAT OPPORTUNITY TO INVITE THEM IN FOR SOME WINE OR CHEESE, AND A READ OF THIS VERY PAMPHLET!

4. INITIATION RITUAL

TO FULLY RECEIVE THE LOVE AND GUIDANCE OF THE HAND, YOU MUST ATTEND THE INITIATION RITUAL. IT IS A SIMPLE AFFAIR INVOLVING A FEW SPORKS, A GOAT AND A PLATE OF CUPCAKES. (PLEASE BRING YOUR OWN CUPCAKES.)

5. RECRUIT A FRIEND!

WE CAN'T STRESS THIS ENOUGH: WE ARE NOT A CULT. DESPITE THIS UNFAIR LABEL PASTED ON TO US BY SOCIETY, WE STRIVE TO CONVEY THAT THE HAND OF TRUTH IS A WAY OF LIFE! THE GREATEST ACT YOU CAN DO FOR THE HAND IS TO ENLIGHTEN YOUR FELLOW PERSON TO THE BEAUTIFUL WAY OF LIFE THAT IS GUIDED BY THE HAND OF TRUTH.

CONGRATULATIONS!
WELCOME TO
THE HAND OF TRUTH

-THE- HAND OF TRUTH

HAT FILMS SEAL OF APPROVAL • HAT FILMS

STUNT LADS LIVE
STUNTS FIRE EXPLOSIONS

HAT FILMS SEAL OF APPROVAL · HAT FILMS SEAL OF APPROVAL ·

WEMBLEY STADIUM

01.07.2020

STUNT LADS

20% OFF YOUR NEXT

MONSTER FRIED CHICKEN

FREE DRUMSTICK!

NUTSO THE NARNA

TICK OFF WITH EVERY PURCHASE!

= ONE FREE PACK!

A SCIENTIST'S OBSERVATIONS ON THE FLUX

What the Flux?!

Despite extended experimentation, I still cannot reach any conclusions on what the Flux is. Basically, it's a purple substance that spreads and affects whatever it touches.

Where is it found?

EVERYWHERE! You never know when you're going to run into the stuff. As a basic rule of thumb, beware the colour purple (especially if you're in a blackcurrant juice factory).

THE FLUX REPORT:
Subject 1/NanoSounds

1. Flux-free

Accident in the workplace! Apprentice NanoSounds has fallen into my laboratory's Flux sphere. Will have to monitor what high levels of Flux exposure can do.

2. 100 Days Later

Clearly displaying symptoms of Flux. A slight taint of the skin and clothes is visible, behaviour changes also apparent. Subject is hearing voices, largely that of Mother. Who is Mother?

3. Current play level

Largely tainted. Kim is gravitating to Flux-tainted abodes and singing nursery rhymes, although she denies this for fear of being locked up in a tower for 100 days. Again.

$$Fl^2 + C + Po^4 = FL^2PCo^4$$

Predicted full
Flux transformation

Will the correlation of Flux match to that of the human genome?

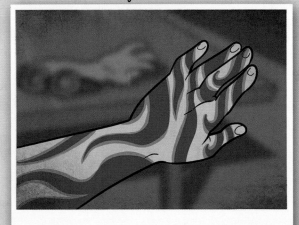

4. Predicted complete transformation

Should infection continue, I have predicted NanoSounds final Flux form. It is frightening. Will she remember me?

5. Flux transferral

Returning to the source of Flux was a bad idea. I am now Fluxed. This was not part of the plan. Send help!

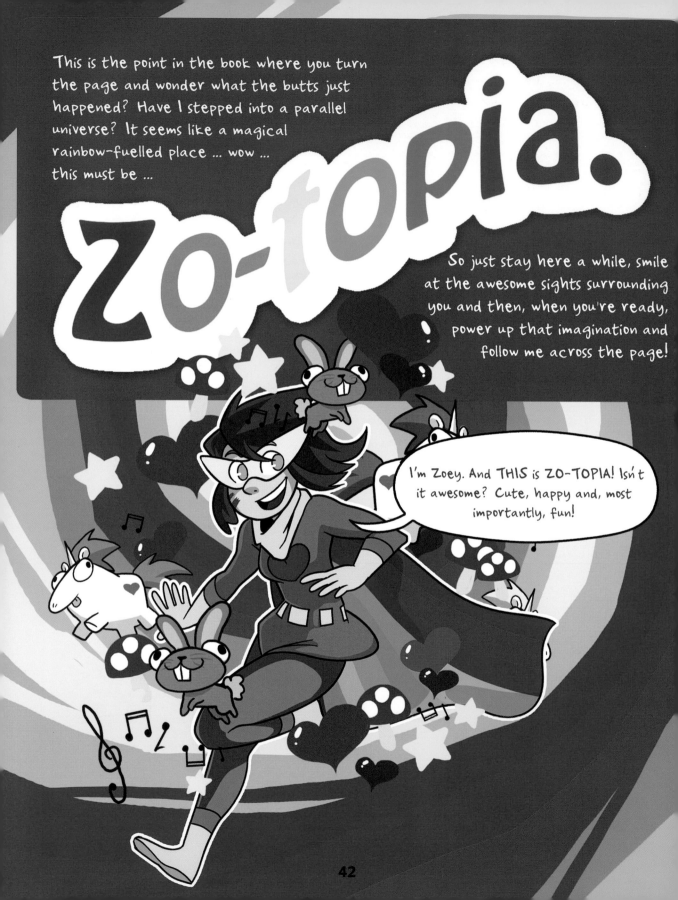

Hey, good lookin'! What's cookin'? Time to get your scribble on. I have a crazy, huge imagination, and drawing stuff makes me happy. Here's your chance to doodle up your day. Just think happy thoughts, then pick up a pencil. Draw the thing that makes you feel happiest!

SJIN'S FARMYARD TIPS

Contrary to popular farming belief, you can actually grow things that aren't chilies! It's not recommended though.

Find a loyal farmhand – a cat, dog, or if none are available, Lewis can be trained to carry out simple tasks.

NEVER attempt to befriend or keep bees. Ever. EVER. EVER EVER.

Chickens are great, but beware if left unattended. They have a habit of multiplying exponentially.

Everything begins with dirt! Make sure you invest in the very finest quality dirt from SipsCo.

SIPSCO DIRT

AN EVENING WITH SIPS

Saxy Time!
To fully enjoy an evening, smooth jazz must be played for at least two hours.

Pledge Your Allegiance
You MUST swear undying allegiance t either Donutsville, Bagelsville or Satansville. And pay your council tax o time.

Feel the Burn
Just in case something, somewhere, actually IS on fire.

PYRION'S AXETIVITIES

"FUN AND AXECITING"

THE QUIZARD

Which "godlike-hero" did Pyrion deal over 49k hero damage on?

What is Pyrion's most played hero? ???

What is Flax's MMR?

Answers~ Zeus, Axe, Blitz's Higher than Blitz's

DRAW BONE KING A DINNER DATE!

SPOT THE DIFFERENCE!

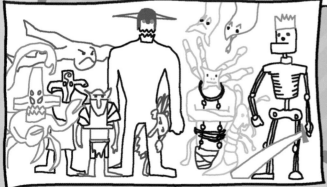

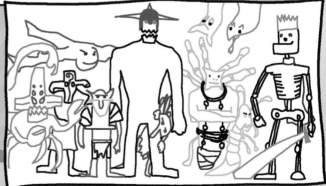

9 TO SPOT! ☐ ☐ ☐ ☐ ☐ ☐ ☐ ☐ ☐

THE FOUNTAIN HOOK

DRAW IN PUDGE'S HOOK

WORD SEARCH!

J	S	R	E	D	I	C	J	P	J	M	W
Z	L	R	H	R	G	U	Q	E	M	W	I
Y	F	D	K	A	N	T	J	E	E	V	X
F	S	N	G	G	X	X	Y	R	V	K	J
W	A	A	L	O	J	E	R	C	Y	D	N
G	I	E	S	N	R	U	E	I	I	V	S
S	Y	Z	B	U	G	W	C	S	M	G	R
R	S	V	A	H	E	P	J	J	O	A	B
A	K	I	E	R	V	X	C	F	T	O	Z
Q	S	O	B	E	D	Y	H	W	C	J	G
S	K	E	L	E	T	O	N	S	T	X	U
J	G	P	G	H	S	T	S	S	J	A	F

NYX NYX NYX

AXE
BUG
CIDERS
CREEP
DRAGON
GANK
GOOSE
JUNGLE
SKELETON
WIZARD

WELCOME TO BLACKROCK CASTLE

Practice makes perfect! It takes time and effort to become a proper mage!

Every mage needs some rest and relaxation. A nice drink with Ravs in the Crooked Caber is always good. The secret ingredient is squid. (Shhh!)

Mushrooms love to chat, but they mostly talk mushroom politics, which can get really boring.

51

WARNING:
YOU ARE NOW BEING TRANSPORTED TO
DATLOF

PLEASE READ THE HEALTH & SAFETY INFORMATION BEFORE LEAVING THE COMFORT OF THIS PAGE.

IF YOU TRAVELLING TO DATLOF WE ASK YOU TO EXERCISE

EXTREME CAUTION

Before travelling, we strongly recommend that you obtain travel insurance which will cover all overseas costs, including emergency evacuation, repatriation of swine and any legal costs. You should check for exclusions and, in particular, that your policy covers you for popular Datlovian activities including taking part in battle enactments.

IF THERE IS AN EMERGENCY, OR IF YOU NEED HELP AND ADVICE, DON'T ASK – JUST RUN.

MAP OF DATLOF

GIN RESERVES

FORMER SITE OF HIGH COMMISSION OF DATLOF

Western Front

MOUSTACHE MUSEUM

ALAN BRINDLEY RIALTO BRIDGE

HISTORIC OLD TOWN

Fern Forest

Lake D

PIG MEAT FACTORY

STATUE OF GLORIOUS LEADER

WHEAT STORES

INFERIOR NATION

Northern Hills

CENTRAL COMPOUND

LEWISGRAD BATTLEFIELDS

CITY OF DATLOF

DATLOFIAN RUBBLE DUNE

IMPERIAL PALAZZO

PUNY POWERLESS NATION

CABBAGE FIELD

TURNIP FIELD

WAR MEMORIAL

PIG FIELDS

The Lowlands

HISTORY OF DATLOF

The glorious nation of Datlof was founded at 5.35 p.m. on the 5th of December in the year 4000 BC by Lewis Brindley, when the experienced and masterful battlefield general was sozzled. He declared himself Mighty Emperor and Supreme Leader of a primitive settlement, which would soon become the proud city of Datlof. Growth was rapid under the productive turnip trade coupled with Brindley's expansionist foreign policies.

Datlof's scholar (there is one, we think) maintains that the city enjoyed its heyday between 500 and 1000 AD, when citizens enjoyed the state's bountiful resources – namely gin, moustaches and tea. Soon, ill-advised aggression and a lack of coherent defence funding led to Datlof coming under a sustained attack. Forces loyal to the Dark Lord Sjin saw Datlof almost razed to the ground.

Attempts to restore the city to its former glory have been largely futile. But this once proud nation still has much to give.

 # VISIT TODAY!

THE FACTS

- The national beverages in Datlof are tea and gin. Tea is drunk only when gin supplies are cut off or diverted uniquely to the Imperial Cellars.

- Datlof's climate is unique, with temperatures rarely climbing above 3°C even in summer. The rainy season lasts from January to December.

- The national anthem consists of only five notes. It is sung at hourly intervals day and night.

THINGS TO DO IN DATLØF

Nº 1 ADMIRE STATUE OF ILLUSTRIOUS LEADER

The first thing any visitor to Datlof MUST do is to make a pilgrimage to the Golden Statue of Our Illustrious Leader.

Please note that it is obligatory to kneel before the statue, place one hand on the heart and pledge allegiance as follows:

GOD BLESS DATLØF AND OUR NOBLE LEADER. DATLØF WILL RISE AGAIN.

Note: to avoid unnecessary arrest, ensure you look directly into the camera placed on the leader's right shoulder as you make your pledge.

Disclaimer: A visit to the glorious motherland in no way hastens death. Recent statistics claiming that the average Datlovian has a life expectancy measured in weeks are to be disregarded (at pain of death).

THINGS TO DO IN DATLOF

№ 2 VISIT BOTH OF BUILDINGS

Datlof has not one, but two remaining edifices and they are well worth a visit!

The first houses the world-famous Datlof Moustache Museum.

MOUSTACHE
MUSEUM

Inside, you'll find the finest collection of moustaches outside Mexico, some still attached to the heads on which they grew. Situated directly beneath the museum, in an underground bomb shelter, is the Bunker Nite Club. As all music, except the national anthem and certain 1987 Eurovision hits, is banned in Datlof, the atmosphere can seem subdued.

Datlof's other remaining building is the Imperial Palazzo.

Forgive the cracked windows and peeling paint, but this structure is the Emperor's private residence. It is said to be papered from floor to ceiling in gold leaf. Note: this is not open to the public.

Our Supreme Leader no longer inhabits the Palazzo; he now chooses to look down on his people from the lofty heights of space. Seriously, he's watching you.

IMPERIAL
PALAZZO

Nº 3 LEARN TO "SWEINJIG"

Pigs are a large part of Datlovian culture. They are revered, celebrated and then quickly consumed. A visit to the Pig Spa and Training Ground, to touch the fabled "Trotter of Torment", is a must. Cut from Datlof's founding swine, legend has it that the trotter will turn to dust if Datlof ever falls.

Speaking of swine, make sure you join in with a traditional Datlovian Pig Dance. These are colourful and unique gatherings held randomly throughout the city, and your participation in a Sweinjig is demanded.

Novices can easily pick up the rudiments by performing the basic movement of an up-down thrust with a rhythmic knee bend, whilst balancing a pig or piglet on their head.

POPULAR SWEINJIG PARLANCE

"Getting jiggy with a piggy" – to attend a dance.

"Bringing home the bacon" – hiding pork in your clothes to eat later.

THINGS TO DO IN DATLOF
Nº 4 MARCH FOR THE MOTHERLAND

The Glorious Motherland March to the Lewisgrad battlefields is another unmissable event. It takes place on the first Tuesday of each month, and leaves from the compound next to Brindley Square, wending its way over the Alan Brindley Rialto Bridge. The march ends with an enactment of the Great Battle for Supremacy. Note that this is an enactment rather than a re-enactment, as this battle hasn't yet happened, and to date any military campaigns have involved the army retreating and hiding. The action can be hard to follow, with uniform-clad participants holding swords aloft and either cowering or running away from the imaginary enemy.

Note: This is an enactment rather than re-enactment. You will be forced into serving in the Datlof Military Manoeuvres, with other uniform-clad participants holding swords aloft and either cowering or running away from imaginary enemies. Uniforms and swords are provided.

Please surrender all travel documents and your civilian clothes to the officials before taking part.

Nº 5 VISIT TRADITIONAL DATLOVIAN FUNERAL PYRE

Having exhausted the list of sightseeing possibilities, surrendered your travel documents and incurred the wrath of our great leader, it is likely that you will never leave Datlof.

A traditional Datlovian funeral is fifth on our list of things to do here!

Flowers:
Floral tributes are discouraged in Datlof. Flowers are considered to lead to excessive and unnecessary merriment.

Setting:
You want your final send-off to be picturesque. Will you choose the tranquillity of the turnip fields? Or, sorry, you have no other options.

Pyre-O-Technics:
Datlof has plenty of wood from the old housing sector. For that extra wow factor add an unexploded bomb or two – there are plenty lying around in the rubble dunes. Va-va-voom!

HALT! PLEASE REMOVE PIG FROM HEAD AND HAND OVER ANY TEA BEFORE LEAVING DATLOF

I HOPE YOU ENJOYED YOUR STAY!

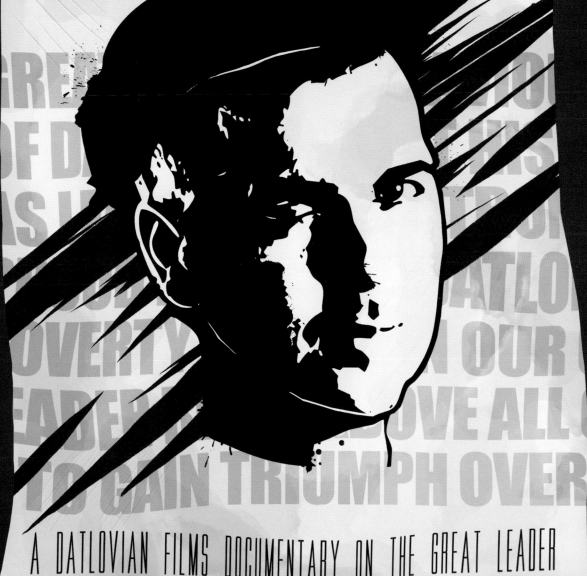

—THE MAN—
BEHIND THE CITY

A DATLOVIAN FILMS DOCUMENTARY ON THE GREAT LEADER

COMING TO A CINEMA NOWHERE NEAR YOU!

YOGLABS
DON'T WORRY ABOUT IT

WARNING:
YOU ARE NOW BEING
TRANSPORTED TO
JAFFA
INDUSTRIES

PLEASE READ THE HEALTH & SAFETY INFORMATION BEFORE LEAVING THE COMFORT OF THIS PAGE.

IF A CHIMP CAN VOYAGE TO SPACE WITH THE AID OF A CRASH HELMET AND A BUNCH OF BANANAS, WHY CAN'T YOU? TURN THE PAGE TO JOIN OUR ELITE CREW OF ASTRONAUTS, GALACTIC SOLDIERS AND SPACE DWARVES.

MISSION TRAINING IS FREE!

Terms and Conditions

· Only negligible brain activity required.
· Pigs permitted.
· Ability to hold space bar when prompted desirable, but not a necessity.

JAFFA Industries cannot be held responsible for the safety of its employees. Pursuit of the space cadet training programme may result in injury, disappointment and death. In fact, it probably will.

Jaffa Industries
The Jaffadome,
Milky Way,
Mildenhall,
United Kingdom

Greetings from JAFFA Industries High Command.
You have taken the first step on your voyage into space to go boldly where thousands, possibly millions, have gone before you.

Training to be a space cadet is both rigorous and difficult. Four gruelling missions must be successfully completed before you can earn your JAFFA Space Agency badge and graduation papers. Only those with average courage and small amounts of dedication will make it.

Our elite team of galactic flight technicians will be on hand to guide you through each stage of astronau(gh)t development. You are advised to follow the (simple) directions provided closely and without hesitation. This will determine whether your quest ends in triumph or epic failure and your eventual DOOM.

Before you move through to the acclimatization pod, ask yourself – are you ready to press the space bar?

It's a big universe out there. JAFFA Industries looks forward to blasting you into it.

Xephos

Xephos, Flight Commander

STEP ON BOARD THE
JAFFACRUISER IV

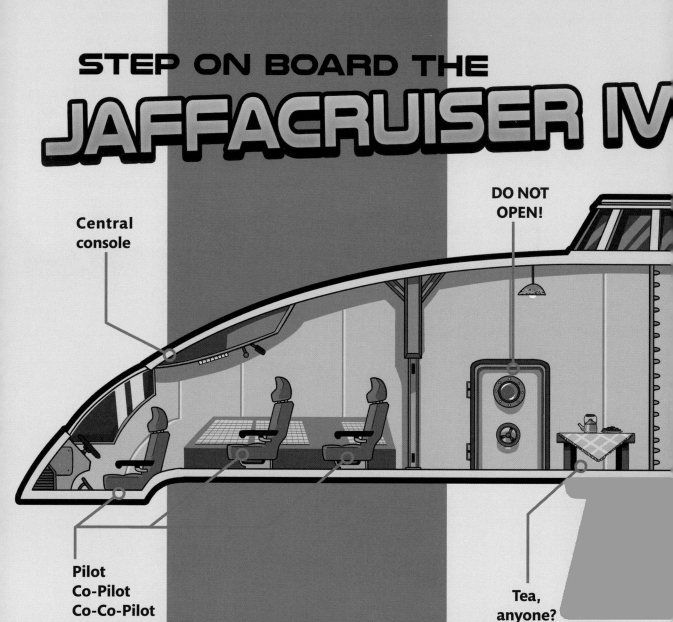

Central console

DO NOT OPEN!

**Pilot
Co-Pilot
Co-Co-Pilot**

Tea, anyone?

Behold the pride of the Jaffa Space Agency, the Jaffacruiser IV! This baby will get you to the Moon and back faster than a slower ship with comparatively few fatalities! While this is nowhere near the kind of vessel you'll be piloting during your exam, it's worthwhile making yourself familiar with the layout and engine configuration.

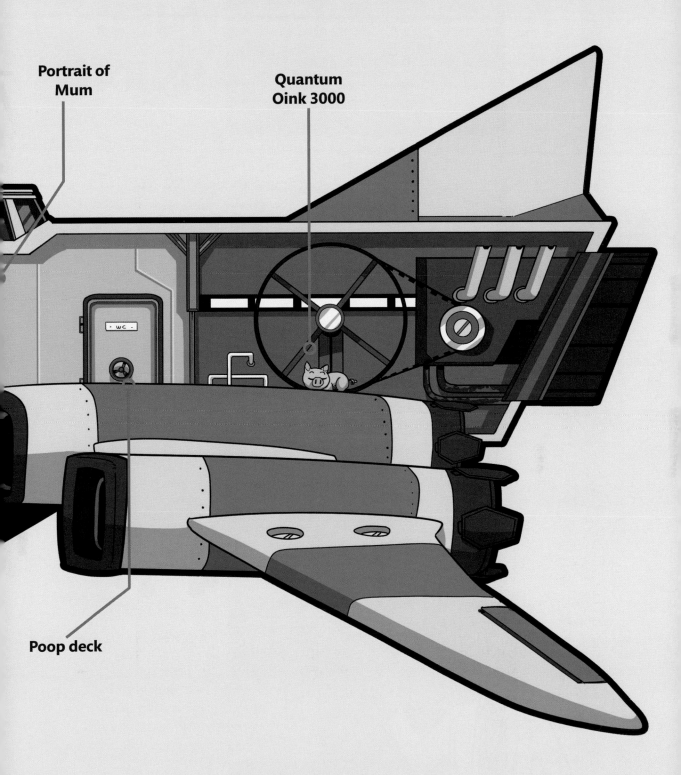

Portrait of Mum

Quantum Oink 3000

Poop deck

MISSION ONE: G-FORCE TRAINING

Cadet, you will need to demonstrate that you have an over **50% PREDICTED LIKELIHOOD OF SURVIVING THE JOURNEY.** Dying during a mission is both costly and inconvenient. All cadets must notch up time in a Reduced Gravity Fixed Wing craft (RGFW). An engineer will carefully control the craft to simulate in-flight g-force.

1 Sit in your seat, put on the harness and click shut the cushioned restraint straps. Pull the straps tight so that your entire head and torso are protected from the effects of 360° movement.

2 If you can't find a harness or restraint straps, say your prayers and assume the take-off position.

3 The engineer will step forward and begin spinning. Hold on tightly and look straight ahead. Do not cry like a baby.

4 Be fully prepared for some unexpected thrust as your seat moves along its flight path.

5 When you reach optimum velocity, the engineer will signal to move forward.

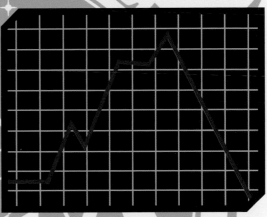

Graph detailing rate of velocity against chair integrity.

WARNING!

As you accelerate you will experience a sense of weightlessness. You will also experience dizziness, headaches and feelings of low self-worth. These are all normal responses, don't worry about it.

You are kidding, right...?!

6 You are now ready to move into the technician phase. The engineer will give you a variety of tasks. These must be executed expediently and without screaming.

7 Once all tasks have been completed remain seated until the chair comes to a gentle stop.

MISSION TWO: AVOID METEORS

In space, asteroids, meteors and comets are an ever-present threat. Lumps of ore can fall from the sky at any given movement. Please note that ORE IS HEAVY. In the event of a meteor shower, protecting JAFFA property is your top priority. Not dying also remains an ongoing appraisal target.

This exercise is dangerous and high risk.

1 Begin to spacewalk slowly from one side of the assessment zone. When you have achieved a satisfactory bounding motion, the meteor shower simulation will begin.

2 An engineer will now bombard you with a range of objects, carefully chosen to resemble space ore. Cushions, pillows and teddy bears are all acceptable dummy rocks. The difference between these and genuine meteor formations is negligible.

3 Maintain your spacewalk until the engineer indicates that the meteor shower simulation is over. DO NOT RETALIATE WITH COUNTER-BOMBARDMENT. You are not cleared for handling dummy space ore.

PLEASE NOTE: You don't need to have an engineer to accomplish this mission. This will however make you an astronaught.

MISSION THREE: FIT SPACE SUIT

An astronaut's flight suit is a highly advanced survival system, designed to withstand any adverse eventuality in space. Your cadet training suit is more rudimentary, but no less effective*. You need to put each of the component parts on efficiently and independently, making use of the inbuilt features.

1 Stand in front of a mirror with your arms by your sides. NOTE: Cadet suits only come in three sizes – small, medium and dwarf.

2 If you need to take a comfort break, take one now. Alternatively, request a space nappy from the JAFFA engineer on duty.

3 Put on the first layer of full body clothing. You will be executing this task in a zero-gravity situation; your movements should be deliberate and contained.

4 Repeat step three at least SIX TIMES. The number of layers worn will be proportional to the amount of protection during a crash landing. NOTE: Profuse sweating is perfectly normal and to be expected.

Mmfghf mmrth mafp...

*PLEASE NOTE: ALL SPACE CADETS ARE RESPONSIBLE FOR PROVIDING THEIR OWN APPROPRIATE CLOTHING. EXCESSIVE CHEST HAIR, METAL SHOULDER PLATES AND HORNED HELMETS ARE NOT DEEMED SUFFICIENT FOR THE EXTREMES OF SPACE TRAVEL.

MISSION FOUR:
PREPARE FOR LANDING

You're ready for a live simulation. Prepare yourself for the ultimate Jaffa Quest challenge. This is the big league. This is what you've been training for. This is the ultimate test of every Space Cadet, the chance to prove your worth. Now is your opportunity to land a mission.

No pressure.

1 Apply pressure to the SPACE BAR.

2 Maintain the pressure.

3 Hold SPACE to slow down!

HOLD SPACE TO SLOW DOWN

Good work, cadet. Only the brightest and the bravest make it this far. You have almost completed your inaugural space mission! Your survival rate is nearly as high as my own.

You are now only one punishing, life-threatening ordeal away from earning your JAFFA astronau(gh)t badge. Just think – your name could be written on the graduation papers opposite! All you have to do is land the rocket safely on the surface of the Moon.

Good luck, cadet. Don't screw up.

JAFFA Industries Space Mining Programme Cadet Scheme

This is to certify that employee

....

has learned how to properly utilize the elusive
and powerful space bar.

The galaxy salutes you!

*Take your badge and wear it with pride on every mission. (Some
illustrious astronauts have even survived two in a row!)*

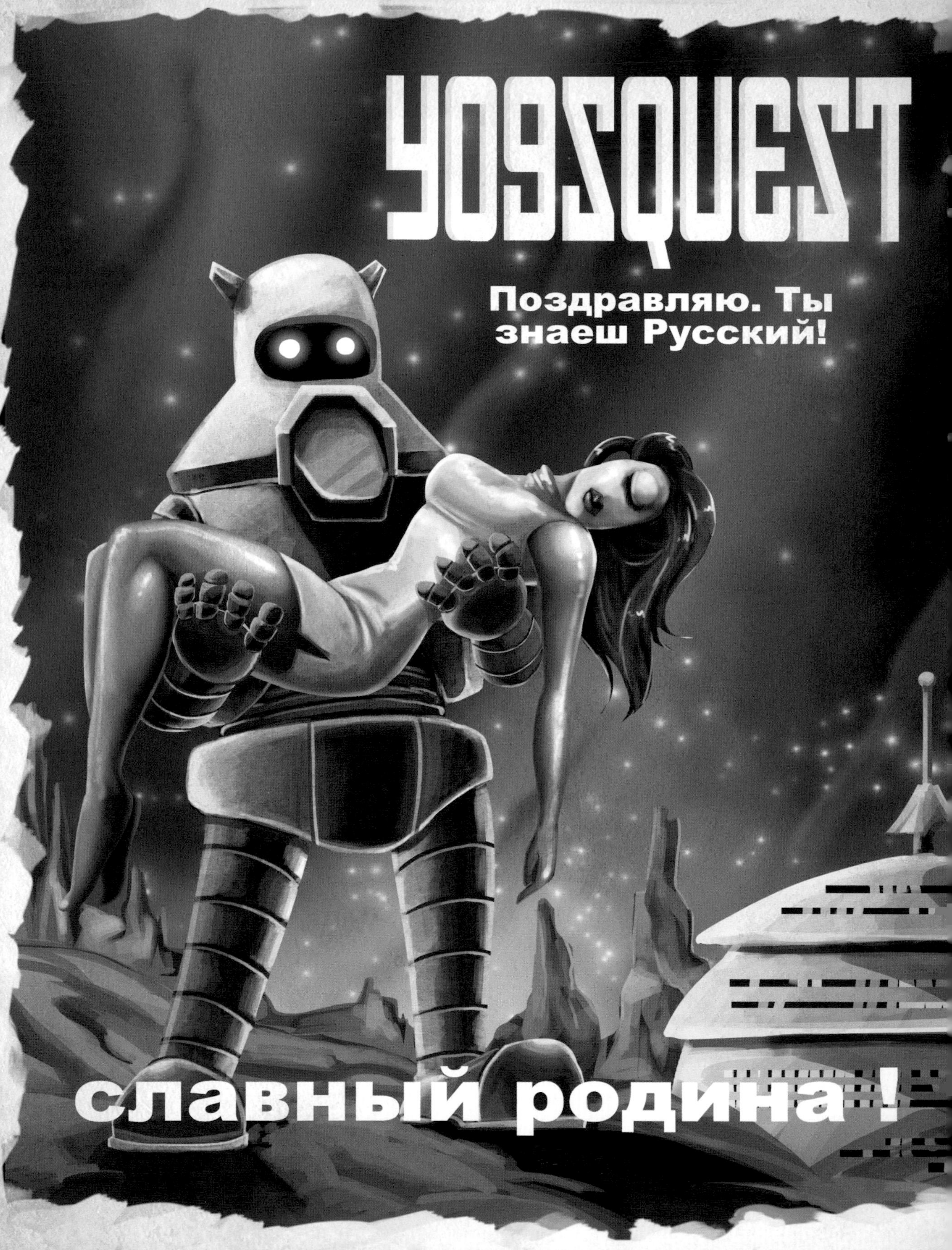
YO9SQUEST
Поздравляю. Ты
знаеш Русский!
славный родина !

"If there's **nothing else on**, I'd definitely go see it"
★★★★
Liam M

"The **closing credits** were **breathtaking**"
★★★★★
Hannah R

"A fully immersive, **comprehensively dismal**
movie experience"
★
John C

"A tale of superior intelligence, alternative civilizations
and impending doom? **I did not see that coming**"
★★★★
Chris T

"A franchise is born. Then **dies a death**. Very quickly"
★★
Kim R

DON'T WORRY ABOUT IT

WARNING: YOU ARE NOW BEING TRANSPORTED TO THE SECRET WORLD OF THE DWARVES

PLEASE READ THE HEALTH & SAFETY INFORMATION BEFORE LEAVING THE COMFORT OF THIS PAGE.

DO YOU LIKE DIRT?
DO YOU LOVE THE DARK?
DO YOU HAVE A BEARD?
EVEN IF YOU SAID NO, READ ON!

For the first time in a thousand generations, the Dwarf King is ready to open the doors to his underground kingdom. Now is your chance to see how the underside live.

The Secret World Of The Dwarves

In a hole in the ground there lived a dwarf.

The dwarf did not live alone. He and his father, and his father's father, and his father's father's father, and his father's father's father's father too belonged to a secret kingdom. Tales of olde remember this realm – a dwelling place hewn into the rock deep, deep, deep, deep, d-e-e-e-e-e-e-p below a jagged mountain peak. It is said that the dwarf and his brethren roamed here in the gloom, fighting, feasting and digging. Always digging.

And so it was for generations.

We mortals could only imagine savouring the dank aroma of mud in your beard and a rusty helmet pressing on your brow ... until now.

The brothers of the mine have made an epic decree. For the first time in a thousand generations, the dwarf king is ready to open the doors to his underground kingdom.

Just a crack.

And for not very long.

Prepare to enter the secret world of the dwarves.

No, you really can't talk about it!

The dwarves are valiant, but they have many enemies. The world below is one plagued by goblins, trolls and unspeakable creatures that creep amongst the shadows. Nowhere is safe. Let this be a warning to you: the last loose-lipped mortal to betray the dwarves was stripped of his axe and banished from the mine for all eternity! The knave was last spotted squinting pathetically outside a job centre in Dagenham with a family of pigeons nesting in his helmet. He never dug a hole again.

Prepare yourself. The terrible truths you are about to read would make a giant tremble.

And so it came to pass that a young dwarf was born. He was Honeydew, noble son of Giblet, son of Gravy, son of Groin, son of Dave. Small of stature (that's saying something for a dwarf) and a curiously high singing voice, he did not have the makings of a great warrior.

Honeydew's heart was true (and he had a well-coiffed, luxuriant ginger beard). But he could dig. Really, really well. Honeydew returned every day, weighed down by diamonds, rubies and gold. The elders slowly began to value their ginger son.

Gold shines and diamonds glitter. Goblins had seen the glint of the gems in the mine. They teemed in the shadows, gathering in terrible numbers. An epic battle ensued and the dwarves were overpowered.

The brutish goblins launched malevolent attacks on their foes where they laboured, in the deepest chasms of the mine. The goblins swarmed down and down, swinging clubs, baring teeth and being generally unpleasant and loud. Then they reached Honeydew's chamber.

Honeydew looked upon the advancing enemy. The humble dwarf lifted his axe and swung. Legend has it that the mine turned scarlet that day. Or at least an eerie shade of orange. The dwarves rallied behind their hero, digging their picks and hatchets into goblin foe. Never again would a goblin, or indeed any other being, descend uninvited into the dwarves' secret kingdom.

Do you like singing in the dark?
Going horn blowing with your mates?
Lurking in holes?

'"Yes," you say? Stand guard! Put your hand on the sacred stone of Khaz Modan. Feel the ancient power of the carvings underneath your fingertips! Repeat the vow three times – once in a solemn whisper, once in a manly baritone, then once in a loud and shrill falsetto.

Only those that make the pledge of secrecy may continue down into the darkened realm of the dwarves.

I, _____

PLEDGE MY UNDYING ALLEGIANCE TO
THE DWARVES OF DIGGY DIGGY HOLE.

I WILL SHY FROM THE SUN, WEAR LEATHER BREECHES
AND LET MY BEARD GROW LOOSE AND FREE.

FROM THIS DAY FORWARD, I WILL HAVE SKIN MADE OF
IRON AND BONES OF STONE! I WILL KEEP THE SECRETS
OF MY BRETHREN.

LIKE A TRUE DWARF, I WILL DIG WITH ALL MY MIGHT
AND LAUGH LOW AND DEEP UNTIL THE WALLS SHAKE.

ALL HAIL TO THE DWARVEN KING!

Quest One: Reveal Your Beard

Every dwarf has a beard. Warriors, pets, women and children pride themselves on the abundance of their chin growths. When it comes to face fur, dwarves are like wizards – the more hair that you have, the wiser you are considered to be.

Dwarf doormen at mead halls and mining festivals are deeply suspicious of anyone who turns up beardless, usually choosing to blindside them with a mace. A bushy beard is not only your passport into these raucous underground feasts, it is vital for your continued survival.*

Your next quest is clear. All would-be dwarves must grow a full and luxuriant beard, by whatever means necessary.

Comb it Forward

Cultivate a comb-over, then keep on growing! Brushing your hair over your face in this way gives you an instantly bushy beard whilst simultaneously hiding your less attractive features. Win-win!

Go to the Dogs

Whistle for your favourite hound, puppy or furry friend, then invite it to sit on your lap. Turn the dog's snout upwards and put your face behind it. Sorted! Look in the mirror and admire your inner dwarf.

ᛁ ᛗᛖ ᛒᛗᚾᚷᛂᚷᚺᛂᚷ ᚠᚱ ᚱᛗ ᚠᛁᚾᛏᚾᛖ ᛈᚱᛋ ᛚᛖᛉᛏᛖᛏ ᛒᛗᚾᛏᚱ ᛁᚺᛁ
ᛂᛏᚱ ᛉᛁᛈᛁᚺᛂᛏᛁᛖᛏ ᚱᛗᛋᚠᛂᛂᛏᛁᛖᛏ ᛂᛚᛈᛗᛁᛋᛗ ᚴᚱᚠᚴᚱᛋᛖᛏ ᛉᛁᛈᛈᛁ

Answer an Ad

Flick to the back of the Sunday papers. They're full of ads for magical hair products. Pick one out at random, order it up, then stick it on your chin – it's bound to work, 100% guaranteed!

Work at a Barbershop

Every time you're asked to sweep the floor, cunningly secrete the hair trimmings in your pocket. Pick up a tube of glue on your way home from work and Dave's your uncle!

Raid a Charity Shop!

Charity shops sell everything, right?

Mooch through your local store on a regular basis. A pre-loved beard is bound to turn up on the shelf one of these days!

*At the last count, there were at least 550 insults in Dwarvish for the follically challenged. All were filthy, most likely blasphemous and absolutely unfit for print.

Quest Two: Find Your Voice

All dwarves and their familiars are fine singers. It is the result of many decades of living with broken volume dials. Dwarves sing when they're eating, sing when they're working and sing when they're ogling treasure. When they're not singing, dwarves are banging drums.

Have you got the voice to be a true dwarf? The gods themselves are said to stop and listen when they hear a rousing rendition of Diggy Diggy Hole. The great melody must be sung harmoniously, proudly and with great gusto.

Quest two awaits. Stand tall, lift your chin, fill your lungs and sing!

Join the choir of ancients, a bloodline of dwarves descending all the way back to mighty King Dave. Use the song sheet on the facing page to channel your inner dwarf.

ᛁ ᛗᛁᛁ ᛒᛗᛁᚠᛏᚷᛁᚷ ᚠᚱ ᚠᛁᛗ ᛈᚢᛁᛏᚢᛁ ᛈᛁᛏ ᛚᛁᛏᛁᚠᛁ ᛒᛗᛁᚢᛏᛁ ᛁᚻᛁ
ᛏᚢᛏᛁ ᛩᛁᛈᛁᚻᛏᛁᚠᛁ ᚱᛗᛜᛏᚢᛏᛁᚠ ᛏᚢᛐᛏᛁᚢᛗ ᚲᚱᚠᚲᚠᛚᚠ ᛩᛁᛈᛈᛁ

Diggy Diggy Hole

Brothers of the mine rejoice,
Swing, swing, swing with me!
Raise your pick and raise your voice!
Sing, sing, sing with me!

Down and down into the deep,
Who knows what we'll find beneath?
Diamonds, rubies, gold and more
Hidden in the mountain store.

Born underground,
Suckled from a teat of stone,
Raised in the dark,
The safety of our mountain home.
Skin made of iron,
Steel in our bones
To dig and dig makes us free,
Come on brothers, sing with me!

Chorus

I am a dwarf and I'm digging a hole,
Diggy diggy hole,
Diggy diggy hole,
I am a dwarf and I'm digging a hole,
Diggy diggy hole,
Digging a hole.

The sunlight will not reach this low,
Deep, deep in the mine,

Never seen the blue moon glow,
Dwarves won't fly so high,
Fill a glass and down some mead,
Stuff your bellies at the feast!
Stumble home and fall asleep,
Dreaming in our mountain keep.

Born underground,
Grown inside a rocky womb,
The earth is our cradle,
The mountain shall become our
tomb,
Face us on the battlefield,
You will meet your doom,
We do not fear what lies beneath,
We can never dig too deep.

Chorus x 2

Born underground,
Suckled from a teat of stone,
Raised in the dark,
The safety of our mountain home.
Skin made of iron,
Steel in our bones
To dig and dig makes us free,
Come on brothers, sing with me!

Chorus x 1

Quest Three:
Dig a Hole

This is it. The ultimate and final quest for all dwarves-in-training. What is the most important thing a dwarf can do for his fellow comrades in the mine?

The time has come. Choose your pickaxe, swing it high, then bring it down into the ore!

Dig, dig, dig, until you can dig no more.

Be at one with the ground, be at one with the dwarves of ages past. When you are finished, satisfy yourself with the greatest reward any dwarf can dream of.

Stand in your hole and admire the view.

Dig A Hole!

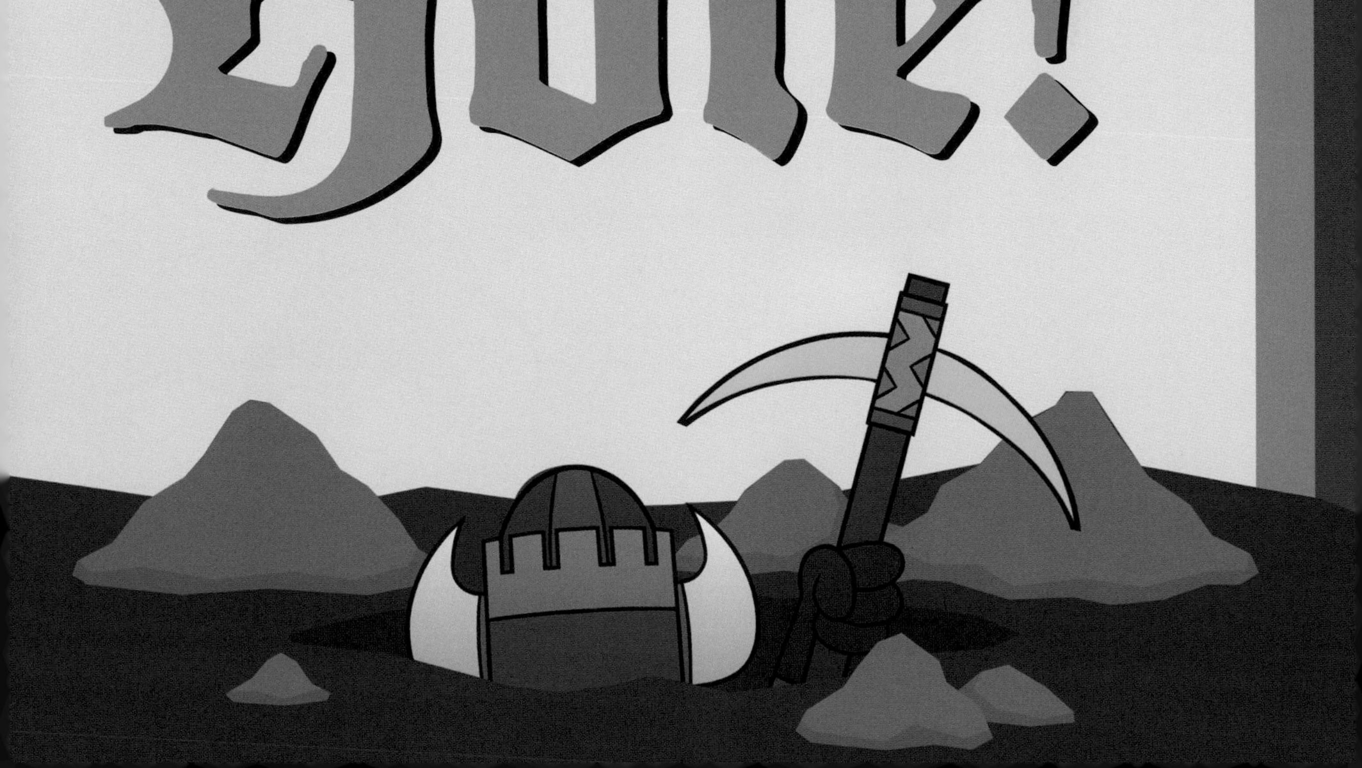

And so it came to pass that a new hero was welcomed into the arms of Honeydew and his kin. Brothers of the mine rejoice! Your quests are over. You are worthy at last to be called "dwarf"! Your lineage has been hewn on these very pages, wrought out of ore using blood, sweat and tears. And mud. There is always mud.

Now your name shall be carved on to the ancient tapestry. From this day onward, the runes will seal your fate. You shall be honoured deep below the mountain peak! Tonight the feasting tables will overflow with mead, suckling pig, sweet honey, potatoes and jaffa cakes.You are ready to slay evil, banish treachery and mine the very bowels of this Earth! Arise, young dwarf. Your clan awaits. Take your dwarvish vestments and wear them with pride.

The horned helmet

The bouffant beard

The metal shoulder plates

YOG DRILL 3000

THIS IS YOG MINE!

SECRET NINJA WIZARD HQ

ISRAPHEL

3 CORGIS

YOUR JOURNEY HAS NOW COME TO AN END

PLEASE VACATE THE YOGLABS BUILDING. DO NOT EXIT THROUGH THE GIFT SHOP, DO NOT PASS GO AND COLLECT ₣200, YOU ARE NOW TRESPASSING. TRESPASSERS WILL BE SHOT, SURVIVORS WILL BE SHOT AGAIN.

(PRACTICALLY)
FREE CASH!

This employee earns
₣200
an hour by partaking
in harmless studies
over at YogLabs.

SIGN UP
d receive the

THE YOGGENHEIM MUSEUM

An internationally renowned art museum, the Yoggenheim Museum is at once a vital cultural experience and an educational institution. View our special exhibition of modern masterpieces and experience the Yoggenheim Museum as an ever-changing institution devoted to the art of today, yesterday and beyond.

A new tale from space! Join the crew of the USS Star Rimmer on their greatest adventure!

"YOGSQUEST"
A YOGSCAST LTD PRODUCTION
STARRING

SIMON LANE, PAUL SYKES, DUNCAN JONES, CHRIS LOVASZ, LEWIS BRINDLEY and REGGIE as himself

WRITTEN BY TOM CLARK EXECUTIVE PRODUCER LEWIS BRINDLEY
PRODUCED BY YOGSCAST LTD EDITED BY TOM BATES
ART DIRECTOR TEUTRON DIRECTED BY TOM CLARK, MARK TURPIN

A YOGSCAST SERIES PG PARENTAL GUIDANCE SUGGESTED
- SOME MATERIAL CONSIDERED UNSUITABLE FOR CARS

Starts when we say so on Youtube, possibly DVD and all your local back-alley cinemas!

YogsQuest

Year 349 of the 6th Cycle
A group of four ragtag people, who are brought together by fate, find themselves plunged into a world of excitement, danger and darkness.

Hatcorp
Minecraftia, Dark Times
This was a dark time in the world where Hatcorp reigned supreme taking anything that they wanted until they were challenged by Team Flux!

Monster Hunters
Minecraftia, Third Moon
Thrown into a new world, adventurers had to battle their way through vicious monsters. It seems a dwarf was often used as a distraction when fighting off the beasts

Billiards
Europe, 1930s
After a tough day working cases, Yogs HQ relax at the bar and enjoy a game or two.

Scholastic Children's Books
An imprint of Scholastic Ltd
Euston House, 24 Eversholt Street, London, NW1 1DB, UK
Registered office: Westfield Road, Southam, Warwickshire, CV47 0RA
SCHOLASTIC and associated logos are trademarks and/or
registered trademarks of Scholastic Inc.

First published in the UK by Scholastic Ltd, 2015

ISBN 978 1407 16399 4

A CIP catalogue record for this book
is available from the British Library.

Printed in Italy
Papers used by Scholastic Children's Books are made
from wood grown in sustainable forests.

1 3 5 7 9 10 8 6 4 2

www.scholastic.co.uk

www.yogscast.com